Animal Antics

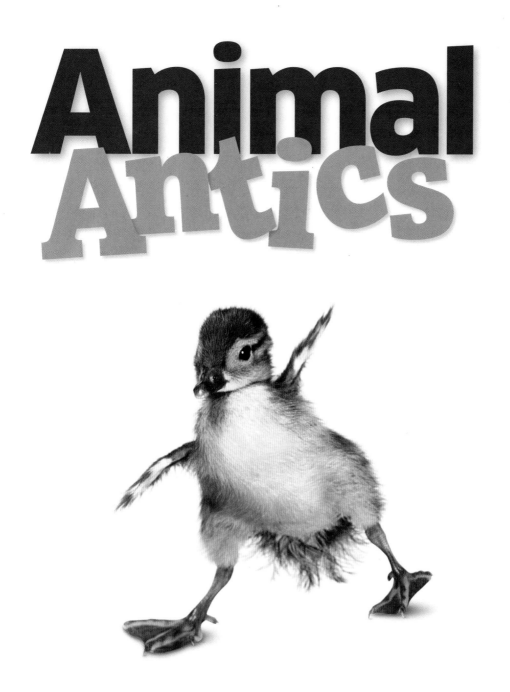

Animal Antics

Derek Harvey

LONDON, NEW YORK, MUNICH, MELBOURNE, AND DELHI

DK LONDON

Senior Editor Wendy Horobin
Senior Art Editor Helen Spencer
Jacket Editor Maud Whatley
Jacket Designer Mark Cavanagh
Jacket Design Development Manager
Sophia MTT
Pre-production Producer
Francesca Wardell
Producer Mary Slater
Managing Editor Angeles Gavira
Managing Art Editor Michelle Baxter
Publishers Sarah Larter, Liz Wheeler
Art Director Philip Ormerod
Associate Publishing Director
Liz Wheeler
Publishing Director Jonathan Metcalf

DK DELHI

Art Editor Divya P R
Senior DTP Designer Neeraj Bhatia
DTP Designer Vishal Bhatia, Syed Md Farhan
Senior Picture Researcher Sumedha Chopra
Managing Editor Rohan Sinha
Managing Art Editor Sudakshina Basu
DTP Manager/CTS Balwant Singh
Production Manager Pankaj Sharma
Jacket Designer Suhita Dharamjit
Senior DTP Designer Harish Aggarwal
Managing Jackets Editor Saloni Singh

First published in 2014 by
Dorling Kindersley Limited
80 Strand, London WC2R 0RL

A Penguin Random House Company

2 4 6 8 10 9 7 5 3 1
001–192973–Oct/2014

A CIP catalogue record for this book is
available from the British Library

ISBN 978-1-4093-5454-3

Printed and bound in China by
Leo Paper Products

Discover more at
www.dk.com

Introduction

Animals can do the funniest things – but when you live life to the fullest, being funny is often something that happens by accident. Some animals can't help doing things that make us smile – whether they mean to or not. We live in a world where a giraffe needs to do the splits whenever it wants a drink – but also where once in a while a surfing penguin misjudges a wave and crashes onto a beach.

Animal Antics shows us the funnier side of stories that are actually all about surviving in the natural world – and the different ways animals manage to do just that. Whether they live in forests or deserts, in oceans or on hillsides, all animals have to keep out of danger and find food to stay alive. Sometimes they simply can't resist taking risks along the way – who would guess that a bird would dare to search for a snack on the head of a hippopotamus, or that a goat would climb to the top of a tree for its lunch? And it's just as well there are so many sensible parents about, because baby animals are often the funniest of them all: watch out for some naughty little meerkats and a monkey with a snowball!

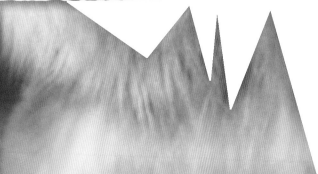

That tickles!

Three cubs can be a handful – or, rather, a bellyful – for a mother cheetah. Mum gets no help from Dad, and raises her young family all by herself.

She moves her cubs to a new hiding place every few days. Cheetah cubs have a mantle of long hairs along their heads and backs that helps them blend into the tall grass of the bush. It takes 18 months for the cubs to learn life's important lessons – including how to hunt for food and how to avoid danger – before they finally leave the care of their mother. The cubs then stay together, learning how to fend for themselves as a group, for a further six months.

Snuggle up!

Company is especially important when you need it to keep you warm. On their own, little bee-eaters would find the early morning too chilly – so they huddle together to keep warm.

As new ones land on the perch they do little side steps until they are tightly packed together, all facing the same way – but with one keeping lookout at the other end. Many birds in the row belong to the same family group. Sometimes they do this when the weather turns dull and cloudy.

I've got it licked

It's bad enough living in a dusty desert, but when you don't have eyelids, getting grit on your eyeballs can be a big problem.

The Namib sand gecko of south-western Africa has a tongue that reaches nicely to do the job. It licks the transparent scale that covers and protects the eye, to keep it moist. Licking is also a vital way to get water. In the cool of the night, dew forms on the lizard and rolls towards its face or is absorbed through its skin.

Large bulb-like eyes

Taking cover
Sand geckos are covered in pinkish-brown scales that help blend them into their desert surroundings. They can burrow into the sand in seconds.

Sand swimmers
These small lizards have webbed feet for "swimming" through fine sand.

Web between the toes

Freewheeling

This praying mantis looks set to go for a long bicycle ride in the country. But take a closer look.

The mantis is actually perched on top of two newly sprouted fiddlehead fern fronds that are just about to unfurl into leafy shoots. Back-to-back, the fronds look like the wheels of a bicycle. The little predator on top is totally focused on finding its next meal – any other insect that comes within striking distance of its "praying" front legs will be caught in an instant and gobbled up.

It's no joke!

Spotted hyenas are very sociable animals – unlike their striped or brown hyena cousins.

They keep in touch with other members of the pack by various calls. When a spotted hyena chatters in company, it can sound just like a human laughing. But you wouldn't want to share a joke with a hyena. As its toothy grin shows, a hyena can deliver a nasty bite. Laughs in hyena language really mean that someone in the pack is feeling a bit scared or unhappy.

Want to know a secret?

It's hard for two young meerkats to have a private conversation. Meerkats live in a big family group, so there is always a babysitter to watch over the youngsters.

When they emerge from the burrow three weeks after birth, baby meerkats have to learn fast about the world around them. Meerkats communicate by various calls, chirrups, purrs, and other sounds. Different sounds have different meanings – warnings about danger or a call to go on a hunt or battle against a rival tribe. Experienced members of the colony can even recognize individuals by their voices.

Having a laugh

Humans are not the only animals that like to get together and have fun. Chimps like to share a joke, and use laughter to strengthen bonds between members of the group.

Chimps also laugh when they are tickled or wrestling with each other. Other members of the ape family – orangutans, bonobos, and gorillas – laugh, too. Their necks, feet, palms, and armpits are extremely ticklish, just like humans. Some things are funny no matter what type of ape you are!

Boo!

The green, funnel-like flower of an arum lily is the perfect pad for an Australian marsh frog – especially if it's near a pond.

Male marsh frogs have muscular front legs, which – when the time comes – they will use to impress the females by taking part in wrestling matches with their fellow pond-dwellers. Their loud call sounds like a tennis ball being hit.

Just a little bit higher...

Elephants pick their leafy lunch with their trunks – but sometimes even a nose the length of a bicycle is not quite long enough to reach the juiciest greenery.

By standing on their hind legs they can stretch a bit more. Elephants need to practise their moves many times before they can keep their balance and get their reward without falling over.

Splash landing

Even the best athlete sometimes takes a fall.

A Gentoo penguin loves nothing better than surfing the waves as it returns from a feeding session out at sea. Speed is important for catching fish and escaping predators – but also when launching out of the water for a quick landing on the beach. The Gentoo's torpedo-shaped body is perfect for these antics – and just for a moment this flightless bird is completely airborne. But sometimes a particularly eager leaper misjudges the landing!

Turbo-charged torpedo
Gentoo penguins are the fastest underwater swimmers of all penguins – and can reach up to 36 km/h (22 mph) when they hit top speed.

Hold still!

Lynx mothers like to keep their offspring clean and tidy, and regularly give them a good licking. They know that thorough grooming is essential to keep a fur coat in peak condition.

Lynxes live in the far north of America, Europe, and Asia. They have thick fur to protect them against the cold, and their broad, padded toes spread out to help them walk on snow and ice. The spiky black tufts on their ears are highly sensitive to vibrations, acting like a second set of whiskers.

I've got my eye on you

Tengmalm's owls live in cold coniferous forests that circle the Arctic, where they nest in old woodpecker holes.

But given a nest box – as here – then they'll set up home there, too. This type of owl is smaller than many others, so a nest hole also serves as good protection from bullying bigger owls – and a safe lookout point.

Funny face

This monkey grasshopper looks as though it's been let loose with the face paint.

In the dappled sunlight of a tropical American forest, its bright colours glow like jewels. If that doesn't warn off nearby predators, then its long, spindly legs are strong enough to help it jump to safety.

Keep smiling!

Living as part of a large herd can be difficult. So a smile can sometimes be just the thing to keep everyone friendly on the open plains of Africa.

Zebras live in social groups and communicate with one another by braying and making different expressions with their faces. A wide, toothy grin shows off the choppers that are so good at plucking juicy grass – but also tells other zebras to keep their distance. Big full-grown males – the stallions – sometimes tussle and may even bite one another. But a smile like this might just stop it getting that far.

Fasten your seatbelts!

We can only imagine how an opossum mum feels when 24 tiny hands and feet are clawing at the hairs on her back.

Opossum babies start their lives inside their mother's pouch. At this time they are just bean-sized, but grow quickly by drinking her rich milk. After just a few months they are too big for the pouch and so another means of getting around is needed. They all climb onto their mother's back and hang on as tightly as they can – wherever she goes.

Fancy footwork

When you have feet as gaudy as these, you want to show them off.

And that's exactly what the male blue-footed booby does to impress the ladies – he struts around waggling first one foot, then the other.

A female will choose to partner up with the male that has the brightest blue: in the world of boobies, a stronger colour means that he will be a stronger father. Their big feet also come in handy for covering their eggs and chicks to keep them warm.

Sneaky supper

Sometimes a wallowing hippopotamus provides more than just a free ride – you may get dinner thrown in, too.

As the hippo rises out of the water, a cheeky cattle egret takes a good look among the water weeds that drape its giant head.

There could be tasty shrimps and worms wriggling about down there. Cattle egrets get their name because they follow big animals and catch the insects and lizards that get disturbed under-hoof. Animals that live in swamps have an added attraction – there could be fish on the menu!

Silly billies

In the dry, scrubby lands of North Africa, desperate measures are sometimes needed to reach food.

For goats, the padded hooves that help them clamber over rocks can be put to good work in reaching the leaves in trees. Goats are expert balancers – but some branches are easier to get to than others. The region's argan trees are like a magnet to the goats because of their tasty olive-like berries. Most goats will attempt to climb even the thinnest of branches of these trees to reach the topmost fruits.

Which way is up?

Like many other tree frogs, Amazon milk frogs have discs on the ends of their toes to help them get a firm grip.

Even the stickiest feet sometimes slip around, especially on the smooth, narrow stems of a jungle plant. Nevertheless, milk frogs are perfectly at home high in the rainforest and even lay their eggs in the pools of rainwater that collect in tree hollows. It means they can raise their family without ever coming down to the ground. They are called milk frogs because their skin oozes a milky fluid that is poisonous to predators if they are threatened.

Look, no paws

Giant panda cubs can't resist playing in trees – even if that means they might end up in unexpected positions.

Mother pandas often leave their cubs alone in the treetops while they go looking for food.

Usually the cubs sleep, but a tree makes an ideal climbing frame. Some keep climbing when they're adults too – either to escape danger or simply to sunbathe. But older – and bulkier – pandas will find it more difficult to find branches that support their weight.

They went that way!

No, this young kangaroo is not really confused about giving directions – he's doing what he can to cool down in the baking heat of the Australian desert.

By licking his forearms – and then rubbing them all over his body – he coats his fur with spit. As it dries in the sun it cools his skin and the blood underneath.

Smile for the camera!

For two young monkeys on the floor of a rainforest, the presence of a cameraman is something you simply can't ignore.

Crested black macaques are found only on the East Asian island of Sulawesi, where they live in troops of up to 20 or so individuals. They spend most of their time on the ground. Like other monkeys, they use facial expressions to help with their communications. But don't be fooled by the cheeky pose – a "smile" like this could actually be a warning!

Keeping it clean

Rolling in the snow is not an inviting prospect for most animals, but sometimes you have no choice.

Polar bears are fabulous swimmers, often travelling great distances to find food. When they come out of the water they shake a lot of water off, but also use the snow as a towel to dry off. The fur of a polar bear might look white – but actually the hairs are hollow and transparent. It pays to keep them in good condition.

Ears are small to reduce heat loss

A warm fur coat
The polar bear is the world's biggest and heaviest bear. Much of its weight comes from its extra thick coat, which traps warm air close to the body.

Treading carefully
Big broad paws are great for walking on slippy snow or paddling through water.

Claws can dig into ice

I'd like a word with you...

A friendly foot on the shoulder is all that's needed to keep things sociable in a group of sun parakeets.

Like other types of parrots, these birds are both brainy and "handy" with their claws. A parrot foot has two toes pointing forwards and two toes back: perfect for grasping at things, whether this is a nut to be cracked or simply something interesting to play with. They also use their beak as a third "hand". Unlike other birds, both parts of the beak are highly movable to give the best grip – useful when you're trying to rip a tough plant to shreds.

Perfect pouncer

It might look as though this fox is playing in the snow – but that's not why it's diving in head-first.

A fox has to eat, especially in the depths of winter, when the voles and mice it usually feeds on are hidden from view by snow. With its excellent sense of hearing it can detect these tiny rodents scurrying about in tunnels they have made beneath the icy blanket – even when it is a metre (3 ft) thick. Once the fox has found one, it leaps in the air and dives right through the snow to hit the target.

Kung-fu Komodo

This baby Komodo is doing its best to look scary by standing up and waving its arms like a martial arts expert.

Young dragons are good climbers and spend most of their time in the safety of trees. When they're fully grown they lose their bright body pattern and turn into huge grey, land-living reptiles: the biggest lizards on Earth.

Spooky squirrel

Is this nosy squirrel getting into the spirit of Halloween, or is something else on her mind?

Perhaps a pumpkin promises an unusual tasty treat? If that's the case, she will be disappointed to find that there's not much left of the juicy flesh. But when you're a squirrel, it's always worth looking!

Getting some shut-eye

You might think it's too cold to get a decent sleep in the icy Arctic – but that doesn't stop a walrus from doing just that.

Walruses can doze practically anywhere: on land or in the water – it's all the same to them. They have even been seen catching forty winks while hanging off the side of an ice floe by their tusks. Some doze off whenever they can – but others can swim about for more than 80 hours at a stretch, meaning they could be record breakers for staying awake.

The mane attraction

Mornings can be a real drag. These five young male lions are in no particular hurry to go anywhere at the start of another day on Africa's Serengeti.

This group of inexperienced buddies – who may or may not be related – stick together and pick up food where they can, even if that means stealing scraps from someone else. When they are old enough and their manes have got bigger and bushier, they might lead their own pride. Then they will leave all the hunting to the females of the group – someone else can get breakfast!

A bear behind

A young brown bear hugs a tree. Is he hiding from something or is he just trying it out for size?

Bear cubs can climb trees – but when they get older, brown bears (unlike black bears) are too heavy to do this – and so spend all their time on the ground. It's useful to know this when you need to escape from an adult male.

I didn't do it!

Leaf-chomping insects are responsible for much of the damage that we see on plants – but not all of it.

On this occasion, the katydid (a type of cricket) peering through a nibbled hole is not guilty. The culprit was probably a hungry snail. Although katydids mainly eat plants, they also enjoy snacking – on snails!

Boy, its hot!

Grey seals – recognized by their long noses – are often seen lounging along the coasts of the North Atlantic Ocean, waving their flippers to stay cool.

They spend a great deal of time at sea, where they are strong swimmers – chasing different kinds of fish and eating up to 5 kg (11 lb) of food a day. During the winter they spend more time on land – where their heavy bodies make them clumsy. This is when they have their pups and moult their old fur. There may be hundreds of seals on the beach, but neighbours keep their distance.

Heads down

When your head is so far from the ground, getting a decent drink of water can be a bit of a problem.

A giraffe's long legs and neck are perfect for eating leaves on the tallest trees, but make it hard to get a drink. Thirsty giraffes must splay their legs outwards so their head and tongue can reach the water. Strong muscles in the gullet push water up into the stomach. Special blood vessels in the neck stop the giraffe from passing out.

Amazing ant–ics

A human weightlifter can lift nearly twice his own weight – but that's nothing compared to an ant.

These red ants haul the young fruiting buds of an acacia tree above their tiny bodies and carry them back to their nest to feed their colony. Ants work together in this way to look after the colony and its egg-producing queen. Each bud is only the size of a peppercorn but is 50 times the weight of the insect. Sticky pads on their feet help stop them falling over while balancing. When it comes to weightlifting, ants are definitely the champions.

Bottom's up!

When your lunch is in a pond, you're sure to end up with your head in the water if you're a hungry duck.

This one is nibbling on the waterweeds that grow just below the surface by sticking its bottom in the air for balance. This trick is called dabbling, and many ducks are so expert at doing it that they get a lot of their food this way. Dabbling ducks are common in ponds where the water is shallow enough for them to reach the weeds. Other kinds of ducks can feed deeper, but need to dive completely below the surface to get their dinner.

Look both ways!

Is this chameleon looking up or down? Actually, it's doing both.

Chameleons are unusual in that their two eyes can move independently of one another: one pointing one way, while the other looks in a different direction. Each eye can swivel through 360 degrees in its conical turret. This gives chameleons good all-round vision for spotting juicy insects – which they catch on the end of a stretchy tongue that shoots out at lightning speed.

Catching some zeds

If you ever see a koala in a tree, the chances are it will be having a snooze.

Koalas eat the leaves of eucalyptus trees, which is why they smell of cough medicine. However, eucalyptus leaves are very tough and it takes a long time to digest them. The best way to help nature take its course is to have a nice long nap while your dinner goes down!

Under my umbrella

There's a lot of growing up to do if you're a baby orangutan – more so than for the baby of any other type of ape.

Living in the rainforest can be a tricky business and a youngster has to learn everything – from how to use a leaf as an umbrella to finding out what things are safe to eat. Mum brings up her baby alone – and the youngster may keep in touch with her until he reaches his teens.

Hands are similar to those of humans, but have longer fingers

Toes can curl to grip objects

King of the swingers
Orangutans have extremely long arms but their legs are short and dumpy. This means that an orangutan feels more at home climbing and swinging through trees than walking on the ground.

Get up and boogie

Polar bears are used to standing up on their hind legs – but you need to steady your balance when you do it in slippery shallows.

Standing tall helps a bear scare off a threat – but also helps it to see further across the Arctic landscape when looking for food or rivals. Polar bears also stand up to gain extra height before they smash down through the snow to find a baby seal in a hidden cave. At its full standing height of more than three metres (10 ft), the polar bear really is the world's biggest land-living carnivore.

Turtle traffic jam

Turtles like nothing better than to bask in the sun, but competition for a narrow muddy bank can result in a pile-up.

Sunshine warms up the body nicely after time spent swimming around in cool swampy waters looking for fish. Back on dry land, each turtle tries to get the best spot for basking. These side-necked turtles have long necks and toad-like heads. They cannot pull their head back into their shell like most land tortoises, but instead can only fold their neck sideways.

Bandit country

In the prairies of North America three young black-footed ferrets peer out from an underground burrow.

Several months before, their parents took over a burrow that was the home of a colony of prairie dogs – a type of large ground squirrel.

The ferrets raised their family here – and used the prairie dogs for food. As the young ferrets grow bigger they will move into neighbouring burrows, before breaking free of the family at the age of three or four months. Black-footed ferrets nearly became extinct, but are now living happily again in the wild.

Parallel parking

You need a good grip when you spend your life clambering through bushes.

Like all insects, a praying mantis has six legs. But only four of them can be used for holding on to stems and twigs. The front pair is needed for grabbing passing prey – and the mantis is armed with vicious claws. That ladybird had better watch out!

Who says I'm scary?

In the Amazon basin, a male jaguar snarls to reveal a set of teeth that show he is the top predator in the rainforest.

Jaguars are perfectly at home in the swampy jungles of South America – where they are as comfortable climbing in trees as they are swimming across creeks. Among the trees, their patterned coat is good camouflage for creeping up on their prey, such as forest pigs and deer.

Three's a crowd

House mice have such tiny bones that they can squeeze through a hole that's barely the width of a pencil.

If their heads can get through, then their highly flexible bodies can, too. A house provides everything mice need: food, warmth, and shelter. Unsurprisingly, this means they can set up home under floorboards, emerging at night to see what the larder has to offer. They are excellent climbers and jumpers, and run very fast. The only evidence they might leave behind is a scatter of tiny black droppings or a nibbled packet of biscuits!

Whoo-hoo are you?

Out on the open grassy plains of South America, an owl on the ground needs to keep his wits about him.

The burrowing owl has long legs for running after rodents, but they also help it see above the long grass. Sometimes it twists its head to get a better look for a juicy mouse or to spot a dangerous predator. There are no tall trees out here, so family life is centred around the next best nesting option: a hole in the ground. An old prairie dog burrow makes an ideal home.

Lion dancing

Play is an important part of growing up if you're a young lion.

These two cubs started out by swiping one another with their paws – but ended up dancing about on two legs. It's all good fun – but it will teach them lessons about how to control and coordinate their movements so that one day they can catch prey on the open grassy plains.

Pucker up

The aptly named rosy-lipped batfish is about as un-fish-like as it is possible to get.

It "stands" on rocky coral using its specially stiffened fins as "legs". Its disc-shaped body is not much use for swimming through open water and instead it chooses to waddle along on the sea floor. It isn't fast enough to chase and catch other fish, so it draws in its prey by using a lure that points forward from the top of its head. Its rosy lips certainly help to attract attention – where does it keep its lipstick?

Eat your greens!

At just nine weeks old, a wolf cub knows little about the big, wide world. For now, it relies on its mother and father for protection and food.

Until it is old enough to travel with the pack, it will spend its time playing near the den – and learn that wolves don't eat grass. In the autumn it will join the grown-ups on hunts, working with the rest of the pack to get food for everybody.

Long legs for running

When I'm calling you...
Adult wolves howl loudly to bring the pack together. Everyone can hear it – even from several miles away.

Fast foodies
Wolves have sharp teeth and a strong bite. They eat fast before other predators steal their kill.

Nose can pick up distant scents

Run for cover

A beach is no fun in drizzly rain, especially when you have babies to look after. With no obvious place of shelter, there is only one thing to do.

This parent plover braves the bad weather while her chicks snuggle under the feathers of her belly, helping to keep them warm and dry. She can have as many as four chicks jostling for space beneath her. Luckily the rain will bring worms to the surface!

Who's laughing now?

Like humans, chimpanzees use facial expressions to show others how they are feeling.

After all, the face is the focus of attention among family and friends. But chimp expressions do not necessarily mean the same as ours: a grinning chimpanzee is feeling rather different from a grinning human being. When a chimp bears its upper teeth and gums, it is not amused, but is nervous or aggressive. If the jaw drops to expose the lower teeth – more like a human frown – the chimp is actually feeling in a laughing mood.

Well caught!

A long bill is good for reaching food – but you then need the skills of a juggler to get it down your throat.

A toucan tosses fruit into the air so it can swallow its meal. Although it looks heavy, a toucan bill is tough, but actually very light because its thin strands of bone are arranged like a foam sponge. The outer layers are made of a substance called keratin, which is also found in hooves and nails. It is often brightly coloured, too. Toucans also have long tongues for catching insects.

When you gotta go...

Deep in the forests of Borneo a tree shrew licks nectar from a pitcher plant.

The pitcher plant sprouts jug-like vessels from the ends of its leaves. Each jug contains fluid for drowning insects, whose bodies feed the plant, but the tree shrew also does its bit. As it enjoys the nectar, it uses the jug as a toilet bowl and its poo provides vital nutrients for the plant.

Just hanging around

Baby opossums love the thrill of dangling upside down from a branch.

They use their hairless tails like an extra foot for holding on to their perch. But the fun of their game won't last. As they get older they'll grow too heavy for their tails to support them in this way. Then the grasping tail will be used for more adult things – such as a brace for climbing through trees and bushes, or even as a way of holding bundles of leaves and sticks for making a nest.

A prickly situation

Ever wished you had never started something? When this bobcat came face to face with a cougar, it had to get away fast.

With the cougar hot on its very short tail, the only safe place was a painfully spiky cactus. Even though the cougar moved off after a few warning growls, the bobcat stayed put. After several hours, he carefully made his way back down without a scratch.

Don't let go!

At just two weeks old, baby harvest mice are already acrobatic.

Their tails are prehensile – meaning they can use them as an extra limb to grasp shoots and twigs, or hang upside down just for fun. Even when fully grown, a harvest mouse could sit comfortably on a teaspoon: it is the smallest rodent in Europe.

Three little pigs

When you live in the woods, a stripy golden coat is good for keeping you hidden – but that does not work well when there's snow all around.

These young wild boars needn't worry: they'll be looked after by their fiercely protective mother for several months – so they can keep snuffling and rooting around under the snow for anything that might make a tasty meal, such as wriggling worms or buried acorns. Even at such a young age, they are experts at sniffing things out – they started rooting when they were just a few days old!

Yogi bear

The big paws of a bear are great for getting food and fighting off danger – but sometimes they are just what you need to enjoy a roll about.

Even when adults, bears can be playful animals. Bears are very curious and will check out any new noise, smell, or object they come across to see if they can eat or play with it. Although most bears live alone, they can form friendships and alliances with other bears in the area.

Brown bears have a noticeable shoulder hump

Long claws are ideal for digging

Flat–footed plodders
Brown bears have flat feet – just like humans. These are good for supporting weight – but not so good for speed. It means that bears can't run as fast as more nimble dogs and cats, which walk on their toes.

It's nippy out!

Even when you're only the size of a thumb, you do your best to scare away intruders. It also helps to have your own suit of armour.

These crayfish normally spend the day in the safety of a muddy burrow – but are sometimes caught out in the open. When danger comes along they stand as tall as they can, waving their pincers in the air. If anyone comes too close, they might get a nasty nip. Crayfish live in rivers and lakes, where during springtime females carry their eggs – looking a bit like a bunch of berries – attached to their bellies. Baby crayfish must fend for themselves – but a sturdy pair of pincers certainly helps.

Glorious mud

An African elephant loves nothing better than to play around in mud – and a long trunk is perfect for making the most mess.

Wet mud cools the body down as it dries. This is important under the baking African sun, where a giant animal is in danger of overheating.

First the elephant sucks the mud into his trunk. Then he blows through it to send a spray of mud into the air. The trunk can be aimed at the hottest parts of the body. Sometimes a naughty elephant just can't resist spraying the mud all around – especially over the other members of his family.

A well-dressed crab

This tiny crab from Hawaii never goes out on the reef without a matching pair of pom-poms.

In fact the pom-poms are even tinier sea anemones, which the crab carefully holds in its claws. The anemones have stinging tentacles and so are perfect for fending off predators that may be swimming around, looking for a snack. The tentacles also trap bits of food – so the crab's pom-poms are not just for defence, but are a dinner plate, too.

Leap frog

Long, springy legs are ideal for playing acrobatic games with a friend.

Red-eyed tree frogs spend much of their time clambering around the tree canopy rather than hopping on the ground. Their green skin colour blends in well with their surroundings. A quick flash of those bright red eyes is often enough to scare off predators.

I'm bushed!

No other big cat is as at home in the trees as much as the leopard: it's an expert climber and is perfectly comfortable taking a doze in the branches after the stress of a day's hunting.

The leopard takes full advantage of its mastery of trees. When it makes a kill, it uses brute strength to haul the carcass upwards. It hides it in the foliage, draped over a bough – well away from the attention of other predators who might try to steal its prize.

Wash and go

Sea otters know that a good wash and brush-up is the key to keeping a fur coat in tiptop condition.

When you spend most of your time in cold ocean waters, a thick coat keeps the chill out – as long as it's clean. Unlike other sea mammals, sea otters don't have much fat under their skin, so they rely totally on their body fur to keep warm. Their coat has more hairs than any other mammal – and their supple body means they can reach all parts with their paws to keep it spotless.

Sashaying sifaka

When you get around by leaping from tree to tree, what do you do when the distance between them is just too big?

The sifaka, a silky-haired lemur from Madagascar – and so called because of its "shi-fak" call – crosses open ground by hopping sideways on two legs. Holding its arms stretched out for balance, it moves with all the expertise and grace of a ballet dancer.

Feed me!

There aren't many birds that can catch as many fish in one go as a pelican.

A large stretchy pouch hangs under its bill to collect its catch when the bird scoops below the surface of the lake. As the water drains away over the sides, the fish are swallowed whole. Although they usually eat fish, pelicans have been known to try other things – turtles, frogs, shrimps, and even the occasional pigeon.

Call of the wild

This marmot might look as though it's bursting into song, but it's more likely to be a male defending his patch.

He reaches up on his hind legs and sounds a loud warning call to protect his grazing territory, females, and family from other males that might invade. A single high-pitched whistle is enough to alert the whole colony to the presence of an intruder.

Beach gymnastics

Elephant seals are amazingly flexible – so much so that they can curl round to touch their tail with their nose.

Their bendy spines mean they can twist and turn quickly in water, when they're chasing fish to eat. Elephant seals are the biggest of all seals, and when this youngster stops growing it could weigh more than a minibus. Adults spend most of their time in water – where they can dive to great depths and hold their breath for more than an hour.

Sensitive whiskers help seals sense prey

Speedy swimmer
The streamlined shape of a seal is ideal for underwater swimming. It doesn't even have ear flaps, so its head is perfectly smooth.

Perfect paddlers
Seal flippers are useless for walking on land, but in the water they are used to steer.

There are nails at the end of the flippers

Old bug-eyes

This tiny tree climber might look like a big-eyed goblin, but it is really a squirrel-sized relative of monkeys and humans.

The tarsier leaps from tree to tree and uses its extra-large eyes to spot insect prey in the gloom of the rainforest. Each eye is as big as its entire brain – and takes up so much room in the head that it has to be in a fixed position. We can roll our eyes around, but a tarsier can't. It means that the tarsier has to twist its whole head around to look in a different direction.

Dressed to impress

Do my antlers look big in this? A red deer stag is proud of his headdress of bracken. For him, the bigger the better.

When male deer want to show off to the ladies they strut about and thrash the undergrowth with their antlers. This builds up strength in the neck muscles. When the time comes, that will be useful in winning antler-to-antler battles with other males – just right for impressing a future mate. Males with many points on their antlers tend to be more successful.

Snake in the sand

For a snake in the open desert, there is only one way to sneak up on prey.

The horned adder buries itself in sand and can sense the movement of lizards scampering about on the surface. When a lizard comes within striking distance, the adder's head shoots out and grabs its dinner.

Old balls, please!

Sometimes a tiny mouse needs a bit of help. Old worn-out tennis balls make a perfect home for harvest mice.

This mouse would usually make its own nest from a bundle of shredded grass attached high up on a reed – but a tennis ball is far safer. The hole is just big enough to let the mouse in – but small enough to keep out dangerous weasels and birds of prey. It means this harvest mouse can raise its family in peace.

The best of mates

The bond between two emperor penguins has to be especially strong if they are going to raise a chick.

They do it in some of the worst conditions imaginable: on the freezing continent of Antarctica. To find their ideal mate, penguins embark on a series of ritual behaviours, including preening their feathers – especially bits that are hard to reach – and mirroring each other's movements.

Happy feet

Penguin feet are specially adapted for standing on ice. As blood flows through the ankle into the foot, its heat is transferred to the blood going back up the leg. This makes the blood in the foot cooler, so less heat is lost.

Claws stop them slipping on ice

Natural duvet

Penguin feathers are very short to help them swim, but they are tightly packed together. They have more feathers than many other birds.

Feeling shy

Clinging behind a water reed, a damselfly would be tricky to spot – if it wasn't for its bulging, widely spaced eyes.

Even its long, thin wings – lying flat along its slender body – are hidden from view. Big eyes are needed for the damselfly to hunt for prey. It skims through the airspace over ponds in bright sunlight, snatching other insects in flight.

Can you do this?

Doing the splits between two reeds is no problem if you spend your whole life on marshy plains.

A female red-winged blackbird (only males have a red wing patch) is quite relaxed as she grasps her perches. Here she will build her nest above water – safely hidden among the reeds from predators, and in the company of dozens of other females of her kind.

A little off the top, sir?

Just about everything in the life of a marine iguana is out of the ordinary.

It is the only lizard that lives in the sea. It swims around the rocky coasts of the Galápagos Islands, where it munches on seaweed and nothing else. The ocean there is so cold that even a cold-blooded reptile gets chilly. So, every now and then the lizard has to return to shore to bask in the warmth of the sun so it can move around again. The Sally Lightfoot crabs are already waiting there to nibble away at the lizard's dead flakes of skin – something the iguana seems to enjoy.

Where's it gone?

A newly born kangaroo is incredibly small – barely the size of a peanut.

It has a lot of growing to do before it can survive on its own, so for the first four months it stays safe inside its mother's pouch. Here she feeds it with her rich milk – and keeps checking that her baby is doing well.

Down came a spider...

With its spindly arms and legs, and long tail, you can see why the spider monkey got its name.

It uses its tail like an extra hand for grasping branches. There is a patch of bare skin at the end that works rather like a sensitive fingertip for giving it a better grip – all the better for swinging through the treetops.

Chilling out

It's usually a lonely life for a polar bear, but sometimes it's good to hang out with your friends.

In the snowy lands of the Arctic you need to be skilful and patient to get enough to eat on your own – a fat seal or a juicy berry – but if there's plenty of food around, why not have a get-together? Groups of polar bears sometimes gather around human rubbish dumps, for instance – and gobble what they can from what has been thrown out of someone's kitchen. When they've filled their bellies, it's time for a rest on the ice.

Cheeky!

Even though his cheeks are bulging, this chipmunk can't resist a few more nibbles of a dropped cracker.

Wild chipmunks usually feast on seeds and nuts as well as plants and insects – but they don't eat them all at once. Some food is collected in their cheek pouches and will be stored back at their burrow, or buried nearby. These larders can keep chipmunks going during cold winters.

Flying floor mop

Is it a bird? Is it a plane? No – this shaggy animal is a dog with dreadlocks.

The Puli is a type of sheepdog from Hungary. It has an amazingly thick, waterproof coat that is drawn out into long, rope-like cords. Despite their heavy coat, Pulis are very agile and can change direction in an instant when chasing intruders.

Bouncing baby

It's not only human kids that like to tumble about with mum. A female bonobo will look after her youngster until it is four years old.

Bonobos are chimp-like apes that are closely related to human beings and live only in the forests of central Africa. They have longer legs and darker faces than chimpanzees and they live in large groups that are more loving and friendly. Some people think that bonobos are particularly good at understanding how other members of the group feel – and will do what they can to keep everyone happy.

Sticking your neck out

If you're a young male giraffe, the best way to show off your strength is with your neck.

Giraffe necks are long and powerful, and when males get together they fight in a spectacular way. With their front legs splayed slightly outwards for balance, each giraffe swings its head and neck and bashes into the other. This can last for up to half an hour – before the weaker one finally gives up. The winner becomes the top male, which means he is more likely to get a mate and become a father.

Singing in the rain

Frogs love a shower of rain – but this one wants to keep his leafy umbrella steady among the falling drops.

A male red-eyed tree frog calls loudly in a downpour – which will attract a female. She will then give him a piggy-back ride for a few hours until they are ready to lay eggs on a leaf that overhangs a pool. When the eggs hatch, the tadpoles fall into the water and live there until they turn into frogs. The little frogs then climb back up for a life in the treetops.

Having a ball

You don't usually see monkeys in snow, but if you go to the far north of Japan you may get caught up in a snowball fight.

Japanese macaques have shaggy coats to keep them warm in a place that is icy for much of the year. In the coldest winters they huddle together for extra heat. This does not stop the youngsters from getting up to mischief, just like monkey babies everywhere. For a cheeky monkey surrounded by snow, the temptation to make and throw snowballs is too much to resist.

Rumble in the jungle

When you're both trying to walk along a narrow twig from opposite directions, who gets right of way?

Two baby veiled chameleons are practising the sort of tussle that will be more serious when they get older. When adult, they will have a more colourful body pattern, including spots or stripes of yellow and blue. These colours will flush even brighter when they get angry or excited – such as when they get into arguments with other chameleons. In the meantime, they can only give each other a fixed stare – and do their best to look cross.

Bad fur day

If you spend a lot of time digging holes in muddy banks, you can expect to get a dirty face and look a little untidy.

This coypu – a rodent that looks like a small beaver – uses its front paws to clear grime away from its fur and eyes. Coypus swim in ponds and creeks, and live in waterside burrows.

Going for a paddle

When you live in a huge colony it's good to have some time alone – and what's nicer than a stroll along the beach?

After spending many months at sea hunting for fish, Magellanic penguins gather on the coasts of South America, where they set up nests in underground burrows, away from the heat of the sun. Every year the male returns to exactly the same burrow and calls out to his female partner – who comes to him because she recognizes his voice. This male and his smaller mate will stay together for many years of chick raising.

Index

Acknowledgments

Dorling Kindersley would like to thank Clare Joyce for design assistance; Susmita Dey for editorial assistance; Claire Bowers and Romaine Werblow for picture research; and Ann Baggaley for proofreading.

The publisher would like to thank the following for their kind permission to reproduce their photographs: (Key: a-above; b-below/bottom; c-centre; f-far; l-left; r-right; t-top)

4-5 Dreamstime.com: Ksenia Raykova (c). **6-7 Ardea**: Ferrero-Labat. **8-9 Photoshot**: Martin Harvey / **NHPA**. **10-11 National News and Pictures**. **12 Caters News Agency**: Eco Suparman. **13 naturepl.com**: Hermann Brehm. **14-15 Getty Images**: Luke Horsten / Moment. **16-17 Getty Images**: Juergen + Christine Sohns / Picture Press. **18 Caters News Agency**: Steven Passlow. **19 Corbis**: David Fettes. **20-21 Getty Images**: Andy Rouse / The Image Bank. **21 Dreamstime.com**: Martingraf (crb). **22-23 Dreamstime.com**: Marina Cano. **24 Alamy Images**: blickwinkel / Peltomaeki. **25 Alamy Images**: Photoshot Holdings Ltd. **26-27 Getty Images**: Heinrich van den Berg. **28-29 Alamy Images**: Rick & Nora Bowers. **30 Dreamstime**.com: Kseniya Ragozina (bl). **30-31 Dreamstime.com**: Martinmark (bc). **31 Dreamstime.com**: Kseniya Ragozina (br). **32-33 Robert Harding Picture Library**: Fritz Poelking / age fotostock. **34-35 Getty Images**: Perry McKenna Photography / Moment. **36-37 FLPA**: Artur Cupak / Imagebroker. **38 Corbis**: Mitsuaki Iwago / Minden Pictures. **39 Corbis**: Jami Tarris. **40-41 naturepl.com**: Anup Shah. **42-43 Corbis**: Alaska Stock. **44-45 Corbis**: Stuart Corlett / Design Pics. **46 Corbis**: Robert Postma / First Light (c). **47 Getty Images**: Robbie George / National Geographic (bc). **48 Caters News Agency**: Woe Hendrick Husin. **49 Caters News Agency**. **50-51 Corbis**: Alaska Stock. **52-53 Solent Picture Desk**: Daniel Dolpire. **54 Solent Picture Desk**: Valtteri Mulkahainen. **55 Caters News Agency**: Steven Passlow. **56-57 Corbis**: Hinrich Baesemann / dpa. **58-59 Corbis**: Denis-Huot / Hemis. **60-61 Caters News Agency**: Eko Adiyanto. **62-63 Dreamstime.com**: Bonita Cheshier. **64 Getty Images**: Jack Milchanowski / age fotostock. **65 Dreamstime.com**: Ongchangwei. **66-67 Corbis**: Anup Shah / Nature Picture Library. **68 naturepl.com**: Steven Kazlowski (bc). **68-69 naturepl.com**: Steven Kazlowski. **69 naturepl.com**: Steven Kazlowski (bc). **70-71 Getty Images**: Michael Sewell Visual Pursuit / Photolibrary. **72-73 Getty Images**: Wendy Shattil and Bob Rozinski / Oxford Scientific. **74 naturepl.com**: Michel Poinsignon. **75 Alamy Images**: Ammit. **76-77 Alamy Images**: blickwinkel / Delpho. **78 Solent Picture Desk**: Henrik Nilsson. **79 Solent Picture Desk**: Jacques Matthysen. **80-81 Getty Images**: Birgitte Wilms / Minden Pictures. **82 Dorling Kindersley**: Jerry Young (bl). **Dreamstime.com**: Sean Donohue (cl). **82-83 Getty Images**: Art Wolfe / The Image Bank. **84-85 Solent Picture Desk**: Michael Millicia. **86 Corbis**: Dlillc. **87 Corbis**: Dlillc. **88 Getty Images**: Visuals Unlimited, Inc. / Gregory / Visuals Unlimited. **89 FLPA**: Chien Lee. **90-91 Corbis**: Ronald Wittek / dpa. **92 Solent Picture Desk**: Curt Fohger. **93 FLPA**: J.-L. Klein and M.-L. Hubert. **94-95 Alamy Images**: Willi Rolfes / Premium Stock Photography GmbH. **96-97 FLPA**: Andre Skonieczny,l / Imagebroker. **97 Dreamstime.com**: Isselee (crb). **98-99 FLPA**: Jasper Doest / Minden Pictures. **100-101 Corbis**: Anup Shah. **102 Alamy Images**: David Fleetham. **103 Caters News Agency**: Mercury Press. **104-105 Robert Harding Picture Library**: Morales / age fotostock. **106-107 Ardea**: Tom + Pat Leeson. **108 Robert Harding Picture Library**: imageBROKER (tl). **108-109 Robert Harding Picture Library**: Michael Runkel. **109 Robert Harding Picture Library**: Arco Images. **110 Getty Images**: Susan Freeman / Flickr. **111 Alamy Images**: Juniors Bildarchiv / F275. **112-113 Robert Harding Picture Library**: Michael Nolan. **114-115 Dreamstime.com**: Vitaly Titov & Maria Sidelnikova. **116 Solent Picture Desk**: Greg Morgan. **117 Corbis**: Martin Harvey. **118-119 Corbis**: Roger Tidman. **120-121 Robert Harding Picture Library**: Michael Nolan. **122 Solent Picture Desk**: Tony Flashman. **123 Corbis**: Arthur Morris. **124-125 Corbis**: Tui De Roy / Minden Pictures. **126 FLPA**: D. Parer & E. Parer-Cook. **127 SuperStock**: Minden Pictures. **128-129 Corbis**: Michio Hoshino / Minden Pictures. **130 Dreamstime.com**: Bruce Shippee. **131 Alamy Images**: Wegler, M. / Juniors Bildarchiv GmbH. **132-133 Corbis**: ZSSD / Minden Pictures. **134-135 Dreamstime.com**: Mogens Trolle. **136 Getty Images**: Michael Durham / Minden Pictures. **137 Getty Images**: mochida1970 / Moment Open. **138-139 Dreamstime.com**: Cathy Keifer. **140 Solent Picture Desk**: Nenad Druzic. **141 PunchStock**: Digital Vision / Keren Su. **142-143 Fotolia**: Eric Isselee (tc)

All other images © Dorling Kindersley
For further information see: **www.dkimages.com**